MCM

CW00509204

Spoken

- word bird -

fourth edition 2022

published by The Poetry Point Press

MCMC Spoken
a.k.a.
Megan Chapman

*Dedicated to my Dad who lives on in his family,
and to all he did and said. You allowed me to be me.*

ISBN 978-173981861-6

9 781739 818616

edited by M. Dunlop

*designed and published by
The Poetry Point Press*

thepoetrypoint.com

table of contents

Foreword

"I have a passion for rhymes and metaphors and writing that identifies with people across class and backgrounds. I want my work to relate to people and give people a voice. I like to see people through their eyes, to give voice to someone who doesn't have one. My aim is to always write clearly and honestly, hoping to reach rather than exclude people. I like political topics on the edge of things, the unsaid, the stories that could otherwise be missed. I don't make myself do it; rather I'm drawn to it." *

Megan Chapman

* extract from "A Space to Write", published by KEAP Cornwall and Tormark Press   ISBN 978-0-9933958-0-2

Acknowledgements

Writing through a dyslexic hand is much harder for me than saying it aloud, therefore this has been a long time coming. Sometimes I feel like i'm participating in the most self indulgent creative form on the planet.

So lastly, thankyou to every set of ears.

Memory Lane

Can I borrow you down memory lane
Everything is so different wana feel the same
Oh brain how I've filled you
Was you to, I grew through
You pursued too much
You were far too out of touch
It's not much I asked of
For me to last and the tasks clog
Was I speaking on behalf of
The dark voices that blast off
When the body stops, I'm the last off
First up, ticking clock, won't stop
Controlling all body function's
Not enough, need some loving
Stop pulling heart strings I'm a function
You're not you're my sanity
No you just gravitate from me
You're not making this easy
It's you who wanted to read me
You breath, feed, keep me
Don't seek me, try solo
I'm dependent, you know so
Well if it's a no go don't listen
Your ammunition words stiffen

My brain's a rag in tatters
Stop pulling me backwards
Stuck to you like the atlas
Forever going round till it shatters

I change grow far from stable
The fable holds a person true
We are products of environment too
Enough contradictions self inflictions
It's significant you're ignorant
Can't concentrate and listen
You never could it's indifferent
My eyes glaze in and haze
No the excuse is the phrase
You've been in my head days
You can keep going I'm amazed

You taught me with mockery
No you control turn the off key
I try, fuck I've tried too
No you do and drag me through
I can't listen to the chatter
It's you who asked what's the matter
Well I'm sick pushed flatter
You can control those thoughts
No your voice of reason haunts
That's the choice you make
No that's my voice you take
How can you hate me I'm you
How can I take having a few

My brains a rag in tatters
Stop pulling me backwards
Stuck to you like the atlas
Forever going round till it shatters

This is not getting easier
Well you got to believe ya
Have control, they're not separate beings
Your body is your mind same skin
The hinge is your mental trap door
Move the ladder you don't need it anymore
The chore can wait you can escape
The OCD can be set free
Don't open that door, it's not easy
An internal plea screams from inside me
Don't tell me this again I count to ten
That second voice fails to mention
I would if I could see I'm lost in the woods
Misunderstood don't tell me I what should
Do a screw loose is the same for most
Walk around daily with an internal ghost
A voice that haunts you judges and budges in
We shut them out but they reappear again
I think back then I think about when
Hold it for a minute in the now not then
It's back that voice of reason 'n reflection
Well if I'm that why the rejection
Cause you fail to answer every question
We are one this is the true lesson   spoken

2

Penryn

I'm from the little old town of Penryn
Where seagulls pick at dustbins
Every bumpkin's rustin'
In salt and sea air

And a time which sits over there
Social media hits a fantasy of glitz
Up the line the big cities in which everyone gives it
The "it's happening everywhere all the time"
Whilst grid locked in lines giving away their time in real time
I see over stimulated minds caught between reshaping 'n define
Tiny fish or big fish choose your line
Mine's a small pond with too few lines
I find rhymes in patterns, unreached mountains
Pipe dreams, river streams, the genie's lantern
chasing gigs, Stig of the dump, throat with a lump,
Writing workshops, festivals, my gigs are mounting

Has it happened yet, I reflect
That snowball effect is subject to bouncing
I'll admit I dip in and out, though writers block has never been about
My writing's uncontrollable, keeps me sane
It's my way of connecting, to give a voice and all of mine a name
Nothing needs to change, found my place where I freely roam
My home is where ASDA trolleys are given new homes
As students comb the quiet streets spending student loans
I feel myself, yes, like I feel it in my bones

In these small streets, like my smell in bed sheets
Life's incomplete when we think of it in uncertainty
Finally I see why I stayed by the sea

mcmc

3

It's me, yes it's me this far out place
Recognisable faces can be hard but so
are hard faces and over populated spaces
Wishing for more races and some more gay friendly places
Again the down side, but there's always sides, marginalised,
fenced in

I meant, there's always been, ways of being, ways of seeing
We all find it hard to understand our belief system
The need to settle in, find a place in
I feel mine within the little old town of Penryn
It's the journey home that reminds me of the joy of where I'm living

Sieving through art keeping the spark close to my heart
Reminds me I'm only ever a train journey apart
I'm from the little old town of Penryn
Where seagulls pick at dustbins
Every bumpkin's rustin'
In salt and sea air

And a time that sits over there...

Pregnancy

Pregnancy what's your take?
How did it happen, what buns in ovens make,
it grates, it burns,
we can't make with no sperm,
but I know that I'm privileged,
cause it's legal and we have third party options for dibs,
but... we still want our kid, of our own,
her eyes and nose, my flesh her toes,
I know, I try to let it go,
waves and pangs mirroring our monthly hormones
old moans, I have googled and googled my phone,
sperm frozen probes,
people try to tell me it's a women's beauty,
but for us that's mixed in cruelty,
third parties join the baby decision party,
my mum's voice cuts wanting to be a granny,
and when we hang with my friend's baby
she gives me eyes wanting one from me,
I'm empty you can't get that from me,
my love and I can't make three,
we see perfect features and teachers in each other,
we offer everything we have, but we can't make each other,
were not chemistry, but were plenty,
I'm pleading with biology,
with guilt knowing it's wrong of me,
our family tree can't throw new seeds,
so don't come at me with your latest baby, testimony chronology
I see friends around me having babies,
I love the sparkle in their eyes and I know why,
but for me it's not as easy in the making
and I carry the weight of lost eyes already here and in need of
saving, out there, in todays terms we have burnt away community,

I know what I feel and I know the connection,
it's not built in blood and skin, but built in rebuilding their bricks of
rejection,

so think careful before you tell us that we have plenty of options in making,
we have basked in contemplation, but I can't take my partner in my womb,
so make room in you mind before you offer your wise words,
cause in truth, in real life were the living flying dodo's
we have considered and withered,
I get it if your offering advise,
but don't give us that bullshit full pitched labour screen
'cause I don't want it if it's not my love's making
I'm untapping the mouths of us all,
this message is written to shared offering to break down every wall,
we don't have the same choice,
I hope in giving us a voice,
we can rejoice in what love we feel and share
words of advice stick as my vice, there's plenty of ways of pulling up the family chair

so maybe not being able to conform will bring its unity,
fluently speaking our futures looking for meaning,
stones are being over turned and pockets burned,
so please don't offer me too much pity,
when you quickly tell us the latest way to try and make our baby.

spoken

6

Death

Oh death you crept in again so silently,
Swept us out of our depths you violently,

Still us forever silenced, your beating black wings,
Never miss a beat, your wicked fate stings,

The eye numbs the heart,
Steals those dearest from whom we should never be apart,

The horse and cart drags across a blue day,
Leaving no trail as another beauty is slain

Taken to a place we can't visit or stay
We pray in whatever way we do

I'm begging this time I'm pleading with you
Stop it, drop it, don't creep in again

Don't take what we love, our nearest,
how dare you help yourself again

Left like a broken stem or a silenced hem
Or a fire dimmed

You've taken the final breath of oxygen
It's never enough for you, you never give in

I'd chase you out of any corner
I'd fight this battle but you just haunt her

Why shut the door on us today
Wait, give us more time fate is a cruel impurity

Leaving those left bereft inflicts the ultimate cruelty
I say let us all go at once, in hand and confidence

Let all our days be filled with all of those we have chosen
Don't take the hands of angels leaving our grip left frozen

Stop, just stop I'll meet you on the track
I'll wrestle you demon I promise you that

You catch another so easily
So why let the air leave she

Wasn't meant to join all the others you've taken
The fallen forever falling, stop with your callings

You take the best too early and spare none unwillingly
You swoop with such unfairness and leave so easily

You take what's not yours, I beg you go easy
You don't need any more but your heartless injustice predictable

You pull off more and more and leave open the door
Death doesn't ignore and it doesn't give in

I'm pleading with you, just leave them,
Change tact, give them back, I already know these tracks,

Familiar pain swells through my living veins
I hear the words, which should never be heard

Uttered in whispers from the nearest of lips sealed in the worst curse
And you with no name leave, I feel the wind again off your back

As black turns the fitting colour, I know you'll forever come back
But in that very moment I find my only real comfort in that.

spoken

8

Eighteen Candles

Back then just didn't know I wouldn't win the battle
Couldn't handle being a handful so I'd fly off the handle
Knowing freedom was round the corner on those eighteen candles
The walls the systems
Lived within my family conditioning
On the bottom of the pile there
I'll write a file on you
Send you on parenting courses watch your every move
On the top it's denial look at what Jimmy Saville could do
The more you have the more you can stab your opposition
Power is power it's a fucked fucked system
So when they've written my title I go outside the lines
Primary school taught me that cause they couldn't shape my mind
Learning how to write letters in between lines
With a dyslexic mind it took me time to find these rhymes
Had a mind which couldn't be catered for in them times
Later these joined up words became my biggest rhyme
Not present in my education
Cause I was bored of getting caught in the trailing tackle
And I'd tackle morals long before this
I just knew I couldn't ignore the injustice
I remember watching a homeless women peeing in a door way
Nose pressed against the glass couldn't look away
I didn't and still don't get why some have and others don't
But I try to process it all chuck out a lyrical rope
Float in a day dream away from the news reams
Cause I see the sadness across banners and stammers
And fuck my social manners never one for matching pajamas
And I know we are all only a stones throw away
Puppets on strings giving this world a play
Whilst a drop away from deaths greedy fists
I find peace in staying present and just doing this

It's a gift and one that could express me
I wanted to share my inner conflict and help others see
Cause if you're anything like me then you're sick of manhandling
And withstanding the age queues and baby taboos
Social conformities and old school dormitories
Please give me air and a chair and my friends
And I will share my chair and all of my friends
See life depends on this and what's good is a gift
So fuck you if you say you can work hard or choose to do shit
As if. If it was that easy then you'd see a version of me
On Jeremey Kyle stripped bare against the TV
It's you and me our world that we see
The judgments and interpretations are natural, let them be
If we can stop turn them off and look inward
Then maybe we could find our reptilian wizard
I shiver I know see it's easier to say than be
So let's stop saying and instead let's see

Back then I just didn't know I wouldn't win the battle
I couldn't handle being a handful so I'd fly off the handle
Knowing freedom was round the corner on those eighteen candles
The walls, the systems
Lived within my family conditioning

ISIS

ISIS have us in tight fists, we can't comprehend these extremists,
Now the global, snowball, show all has subject,
Innocent people, one religion as the threat,
Easier to project than look inwardly- see,
I regret every ignorant word I hear,
As usual they boil up from the same fear,
Generalising, flower bunching us and them nothing's,
With regret yet again I see stereotyping,
We judge one as all it's easier to hide
in Daily Mail branding, news sampling,
See it doesn't look like that from where I'm standing,
The hierarchy's chucked the towel in,
Every EU member's got a hand in,
Planes will bomb their bloody stamps in,
Then charity's feed them, let's give birth then bleed them,
Let's stop charities floating in hope,
Until a young boy hits media's heart strings note,

Sharks drag their prey under we're no different, still I wonder
Who is all this war for, not sure what I stand for

Politicians rounding up and grounding,
British stags rap their wings like shags,
Easy shags, the deflated and uneducated
as anticipated the scapegoat's plated
Up and fucked, the sharp knife,
of slices cut, as we wipe off,
Innocents, like they were never needed, as bombs hit innocents bled out,
Like they never had a life of, a life which get more swipes than likes,
On the underground straight from the killer's swipe,
Buckingham, Downing Street and such like,
Still the government deludes we're protecting you,
We're branded, sanded put into a box,
If you cannot fit it then fuck it - you've lost,
At whose cost? Who's really looking out for who?
It's the world's truth: humans are cruel

Sharks drag their prey under we're no different, still I wonder
Who is all this war for, not sure what I stand for

I'm not trusting in these elite voiceless sheep
Once again the alleged good as effective as talking in their sleep,
If your family lived there would you still chuck, fire balls on oil pools
Or forget it all whilst your family chuck bowling balls?
But you're no fool I see you just like me
and he like she and she like she, accept our mouths taped c'est la vie,

But really as I unpick the news drip,
I just feel better off like this,
The world is shit, so shit it's painful,
turn my back it's shameful,
Wrestle with reality, shove it in a box,
This goes out to the frosted voices,
The horsed and those that feel it's pointless,
So why do we accept our mouths,
Or retaliate with the same hate,
Or worst share the racist, anti-Muslim Facebook updates,
Or knock down the mosque, that's the defaced look,
Through fear you smear your shit like trauma,
Head online, feed the powerless conformer,
Gun them down and chase them to the border,
Fox hunting's back, the new world order.

Through fear you smear your shit like trauma
Head online, feed the powerless conformer,
Gun them down and chase them to the border,
Fox hunting's back, the new world order.

Man and Ocean

You can take the sea away from me,
But you can't take me, out of the sea.

Time Stops,
Over Falmouth's docks,
Flickering first light,
Dance in blues and pure whites,
Sun light projection,
No 3G no be, she,
Is as free as black backed gulls,
hovering weightless above hulls,
Water meets fresh paint slapping,
The breeze feeds
Sheets, withering the metal sings;
[No car keys
No screen reads
No news feeds
No answer no need
No buffering
No suffering
No nothings].

The winds are answering the presence,
In words, letters, every essence,
Sit like sand particles,
So small yet part of all,
Timeless in a mind
Less full, dropping tide lines,
Words pool, the odd message bottled in,
Water tight and floating,
Absorbed in waves like sun rays,
In the Cornish shores of today,
In the unknown of tomorrow,
Mother nature comes and goes,
Let it moan and comb,
Paves the way spitting sea foam,
Let my drone outlive the drones,
AP and phones, Keep your picture,
This Cornish 'scapes too wild, too beautiful to fixture.

mcmc

Let sea salt crystallise tongue ties,
Untie your ties, unify!
We have more in common than divides,
One sky, one tide,
Lows and highs,
A forever changing tide line,
Traced before and after our times,
In a time of such depth and fear,
Tears and uncertainty steered
By the beast which we can never tame,
Ocean and man I fear are one of the same,
I say raise up your Cornish flagon!
You can't rein in, so at times
I choose drink to with the dragon.

spoken

Europe

People people look at what we've done
boxed into a corner politicians behind the gun
I don't fully understand, like the Queen song 'mama, just killed a
man'
Oh man who smelt fear and filled in the gaps
Let beer run freely, pulled up the matt
Tapped into that stupid whispering
Let the pigtails rule in kindergarden
Beg your pardon if I'm speaking out of term
But I'm a poet my dear and I need my turn
My words burn holes in souls
So put on your socks or walk outside the box
See now ...
Fear grew fear grew fear,
If that's all your hear, then that's what steers
uneducated is dangerous mixed with hatred
Misrepresented, looking for a matrix
Of course they pointed off the map
Like blind murder, in real life daily mail feeds or observer,
Reading through fear, gave you a heart beat ,
Gave out a vote, sealed with lies and false hopes,
Social uncertainty, on your knees, happily receives an antidote,
Gave it to our people who should never of been roped
In with fear, working off a false political revolt
Smoke signal ideal, tapped into how we feel,
Like cereal adverts, empty consumers splurge
Out at all costs, advertisement pulls out the stops
Voices echo, adopt, out not in, but we never new the costs
Lost leading the blind, how the fuck can we define
Finances, history the EU's blood line
You didn't answer mine I said stay in
Ever since I've been apologising
Dreading the next time I change the pound
It's a fucked land now, that's insignificant to the profound
Ways are countries have been glazed 'n grown a back bone
There's been friction, but we had shared a home
Unity, in it together across the sea
I'm not sure what, don't follow political plots
But I shared the ideals, wanted to stay in with them lot
Why ask us at a time of such desperation

spoken

We're so right winged it's disabling
For the disabled it's crippling
The media's got us dribbling
Round cones with their moans, people don't see it
Controlled by the fear and the ignorance that steers this
At what cost we brexist the same fear, please pull yourself back in
European is a good thing, stop all the hating
If you don't understand don't fill in the gaps
That's bad communication, which first snowballed, fools with this crap
Britain hatched out of the ashes, which we've already scattered
Across bloodied fields, don't lost lives matter

Instead we batter each other, re-dig the trench
Check in refugees, rip up the fence
What's meant to be we when we fuck our children's destiny
Rip off the Union Jack like a fresh bikini wax
Max out our finances, clamp down our borders
We're raw with sores, this new worlds deformed us
On the plus we can jump higher up American's back
Let the bully continue cruelty, as politicians currently hatch out
Arguably the scariest leaders I've ever seen
Fuck politics 'n media's blundering
Let this poem revolt, role in and out like thunder
The lightening's already struck I predict a blunder
I say grab the bull by the horns before this deforms us
Share community visions, sign partitions rise out the dust
Stand shoulder to shoulder like Stonehenge boulders
Countries depend on each other and our waters

A core of sandy shores worth more than what defines our borders

See Your

See the pain pinned up on your face,
See the difference that you make,
See you listen and you wait,
See what someone already take,
See the snake wrapped around your neck,
See the tape draped across the desk,
See the dead body you won't forget,
See those eyes you've never met,
See that lost soul you project,
See your tossed body you forget,
See a version of your person,
See your deserving tried still learning,
See the unearthing and talking,
See the disturbing paths you're walking,
See your story through your lens,
See your gory see your trends,
See your confidential and potential,
See your trade mark and strong heart,
See you embark in dark paths,
See your path was never lite,
See a candle born with no wick,
See the covered mothered in pain
See the uncovered wearing their parents shame,
See a spinning weather vein,
See your sinning is your claim,
See you're caught up in a web,
See your self taught head,
See your dread and your fears,
See your tears as I hear,
See your life,
See your day,
See your kite, please fly today

Dad

Dad the one who sprung and begun me
I swung off every word he nurtured me
Walked and crawled, played ball
As I grew up he helped me stand tall
The fool and wisdom of words
'Cause if he didn't know he'd look
He took the dictionary down for me
At every point he grounded me selflessly
His body language was always real
If uncomfortable he showed me that's no big deal
Could tell him any thoughts and feelings, always okay
Able to say, relationships to anything, anything
No sensors, now gone I know what he'd be saying
Spider keep your head up this sorrow will drown you
Life's not for ever I'm just happy I found you
So dad I now have to make up a new wish list
I had my wish for four years so I guess
This life is as temporary as you always told me
I never imagined a life now as empty
You gave me plenty, never enough; still I'll remain tough

Taught me more than life itself
Taught me how to be myself

You're a true legend, thanks for being my friend
I now appreciate the brush of your paintings
Before I found them hard to relate in
It's an art form like this I just wish
I could see you again, give you a kiss
Sit in silence and pass the time of day
Catch you unexpected in the garden, say
Cup of tea, no, stay where you are
Talk to you about my latest cheap car
Hear your most recent sailing tactics
Tell you about my surf or latest performance

You used to always leave my bedroom door ajar
Tuck me in, then when I grew up, let me walk out far
You are so special and cannot be forgotten
I just miss you so much it feels physical, want to update you
with what's on
So I'll just close my eyes and see you
I'm temporarily frozen, you gave me your preview
See you in so many new and old memories
Happy back then, you knew what you meant to me

Taught me more than life itself
Taught me how to be myself

From my life to your death you were my safety net
Now life's jumped you, I'll wait, I'm not done yet
Regret is a word which is so absurd
I will deflect it and make my own proverbs
You're the wax in every candle, every grain of sand in my
sandals
I feel you in every breath you are me
There is so much left without you to see
I wanna be next to you, I miss you deeply
It's not easy the more time without you scares me
I don't want any of my memories to fail so empty
Meg remember dad's the wind in the sails when it's breezy
You're my November you are my friend forever
I can't pretend the days will ever be the same
You were the one in every billion, thanks a million
And you've been irreplaceable
Rest assure I'll cope, before wasn't imaginable
I just hope where you are does you justice
You're in our hearts and minds amongst us
So long life I will follow his track
Just hope when I go I'll get you back

Taught me more than life itself
Taught me how to be myself

"McMcSpoken (Meg Chapman) is a spoken word artist of real honesty speaking from the heart and taking on personal and political subjects. From her days at Dartington College of Arts through to her current arts workshops and all the energetic raw performances in between; to see and hear Meg's work is to know Meg ,it's all real. With a hip hop flair and stream of consciousness style, Meg is a stellar performer and a downright lovely woman to boot!"

Gina Sherman, Apples and Snakes, SW Producer

"Meg Chapman (MCMC Spoken) delivers powerful, often hard-hitting pieces, rich in social commentary and humanity.

Des Hannigan, journalist and travel writer

"Beautifully constructed politically potent poetry with rhythm at its heart. MCMC Spoken creates warmth from the moment she steps on stage and her humanity is written into every poem she performs."

Sara Hirsch

mcmc   spoken mcmc

spoken

MCMC Spoken a.k.a. Megan Chapman - links to live recordings:

See Your
 www.youtube.com/watch?v=p3wwOw5x22A
BBC commissioned piece
 www.youtube.com/watch?v=M-_1dV44PFg

contact information:

Megan Chapman
email: mcmcspoken1@gmail.com
instagram: mcmc_spoken
Facebook or You Tube: MCMCSPOKEN
twitter: @MCMCSpoken
website: www.mcmcchapman.wixsite.com/mcmc
soundcloud: www.soundcloud.com/mcmcspoken

The Poetry Point Press is an in-house editing, design and publishing service.

To find out more email: *macd@cubecinema.com*

thepoetrypoint.wordpress.com